Meredith!
Let me know what
you think about
cget after fitness!

♡ Rhye Sy

Self Help Guide

to GAF

Dedicated to my Mom

*Thank you for always
believing in my vision.*

Dear you,

This is it. You've picked up this book looking for some type of inspiration or a reason to **GAF** (Give a F*%$) a little bit more in some area of your life I. Got. You.

We're going to comb through several aspects of your life and recharge you. I hope to bring you some fresh perspective that also keeps it real. From money to health to a rejuvenated mentality, you're about to LEVEL UP.

There were several times in my life where I had to step back and reinvest in myself, challenge myself, push myself. That's what I want to do for you. Success! I found my success, my life, my mind elevated and stayed consistently on the rise when I really started to **GAF**! In an organized and real way.

I can't say that I'm Warren Buffett or Oprah but the success I have continues to blossom and I want people to win as much as I have.

Each chapter before your think space has a **GAF** theme to keep you motivated and reminded that we are playing no games! Let's get started. This is a journal for YOU, with some motivation from ME. Let's do this!

GAF = GET ALL FINANCES

Get all of your finances and I mean ALL of them and write them down here; from rent to how much you spend on your dog's food every month! Detail it out honey and total it up!

_____
_____
_____
_____
_____
_____
_____
_____
_____
_____
_____
_____
_____
_____
_____
_____
_____
_____
_____
_____
_____
_____
_____
_____

So, what's up?

If this total is more than two paychecks, then what are you doing? You know what my mom ALWAYS told me? "Live in your means." Don't be out here trying to have a champagne lifestyle on a beer budget. Be real with yourself. If this is not reflective of your paychecks where can you cut cost? Here are a few suggestions...

Rent

Is rent pretty much a full paycheck? Then that's too much, size it down to a third of your monthly income or less. If you already signed a lease try to negotiate with your manager about extending the lease for less payment per month. Yes, you can negotiate rent price (and damn near anything) and don't be afraid to! If you're on your way out of a lease keep the "third rule" in your head and that includes UTILITY COSTS.

Go to the store

I mean really, like make a list and everything, you have several pages to do that! But we'll dive deeper into this a little later.

Download a finance app

Download an app that can link to your bank account and track all of your finances. You're probably not as "woke" as you think you are about how much you spend on lattes and vegan pizza. If I triggered you with that last sentence... I'm not sorry. The Mint App is an example of a good tracking tool and helps you track your **CREDIT** and how in the world you're spending your money. Using an app like this helped me realize just how much I was spending on food/take out. It also helped me recalibrate that spending on meal prep instead.

Your credit is IMPORTANT

Stop ignoring or not checking your credit! (If you do check it, then great). You need good credit for essentially everything! Opening new accounts, cars, LOW APR (Annual Percentage Rate). The better your credit the lower your bills can be, but do you hear me though? Work on it and keep going! There can be old accounts and history affecting your credit score that you can fix, but you won't know there's a problem, until you actually check it. Credit Karma is a good resource for that. Both of the apps I mentioned will allow you to check your score frequently and without penalty.
You have an Equifax, Experian and TransUnion score. The highest will usually be your TransUnion score. Companies will use that score to determine your APR if you're trying to buy or refinance something. You should be able to recite your credit score like you can your phone number. I check my score on a weekly basis.

By checking my credit

I've been able to clear old accounts or settle inaccurate information that has increased my credit score. Don't be afraid to do that either. Credit Karma will help you dispute inaccurate information with a click of a button. I've also contacted companies directly to tell them how they've negatively affected my credit score and if they reported inaccurate information – GAF, it's worth it!!

PAY THOSE BILLS ON TIME!

Late fees can add up to groceries or go toward your light bill. Use the next couple of pages to go through all your bills and write out the due date for each one. If you write it down and continuously see it, it'll reinforce the urgency of paying the bill and the consequence if you don't. I dare say, you might even pay early.

STUDENT LOANS (If this doesn't apply to you I'm jealous, but go ahead and skip this)

Whewwwww. Yeah. I'll keep this one quick because at the end of the day we have to pay them. I've somehow had success in balancing out student loans by calling, actually calling the company I've borrowed from, updating them on where I'm at financially and what I can afford. The call has taken time out of my day, BUT in the end, I communicated and it usually results in a better plan to make payments. If you stay on the phone long enough, eventually, you will run into someone who cares. :)

If your credit is high enough and your debt to income ratio meets requirements you can refinance your loans. There are companies that help you through this process. I will tell you that it's harder if your loan debt is six digits, but that doesn't mean it's impossible. Ask for help, talk to people about your options, and don't just submit any application electronically. If the application doesn't go through, ask why and work that into your new goals, while getting information on other options.

Exercise: **Write down three or more bills right now that you can change, take out or lower! A good start is going back and flipping through all of your subscriptions. Do you really need five streaming services? Probably not. You can save that money and put it towards another bill. Keep track of where that money is going and how you can use it more efficiently in the next few pages.**

_____
_____
_____
_____
_____
_____
_____
_____
_____
_____
_____
_____
_____
_____
_____
_____
_____
_____
_____

_____

_____

_____

_____

_____

_____

_____

_____

_____

_____

_____

"I got a couple past due bills I won't get specific, I got a problem with spending before I get it." – Kanye West

_____

_____

_____

_____

_____

_____

_____

_____

_____

_____

_____

_____

_____

_____

_____

GAF = GET ALL FOOD

Get all the food you've eaten in the last week (try to remember) and write down next to it how much you paid.

Listen, unless you're a millionaire you are seriously trippin' if you're eating out every day or every other day. I'm pretty sure millionaires also pay someone to go get their GROCERIES. If Bill Gates is happily making and eating peanut butter sandwiches at home, then you'll be ok too. SOOOo let's make eating out more of a treat instead of habit. I get it some days you're just tired. I can guarantee that if you start eating and making healthier meals at home you'll become more conscious financially and nutritionally about how you get and have food in your life, which brings me to my next point.

Food is nourishment and energy! **GAF** about what you're eating! Even if you do pop it in the oven or you're challenged in the kitchen; grabbing more vegetables and fruit you can pick up and eat are going to keep your energy going and you more focused.

A couple of tasty tidbits
Read the label and the servings - UHM HELLO I was surprised by how many people don't do this **correctly** or at all! Everything is broken

down by servings but then you have to do a little math, it's going to be ok.

A majority of package goods will tell you the calories **PER SERVING SIZE**. Somewhere near it will be the **number of total servings** in the entire package and then you have to multiply it.

Example: If Hot Chips have **210 calories** per serving and the **SERVING SIZE** on the bag says **three**:
Then the entire bag is 210 x 3 = 630 calories
(This is not an accurate depiction of how many actual calories are in hot chips).

K? k. So I'll leave how much you've really been eating between you and the bags, moving forward, let's make sure you're running those numbers.

Get snacks!
It's ok to snack, when it's healthy. Protein clusters, fruit and nutrition bars are a lifesaver, especially when you're on the go. There are so many healthy alternatives out there now. If you're a nervous eater or just a muncher then you have to make more of a conscious effort about what you're picking up. Find yourself

eating pretzels or chips? You probably like crunch; maybe coconut clusters or carrots would be a good sub out. Cookies? There are delicious vegan snack bars out there that are sweet, filling, and a lot healthier than a cookie.

Write out a menu for the week!

I love doing this. This is not only a plan but if feels more like self-care. When you're done making your menu, that store run will be a lot easier because you know what you're eating for the week. Writing it down also adds that element of accountability.

Does life happen and you might miss a day or two from your menu? **YES HONEY,** but you'll ultimately feel better that you did it for you to begin with! My plans are usually for five times out of the week to leave some weekend wiggle room. It's up to you on how creative you want to be.

Three ingredient meals

You can throw in the skillet with a little olive oil salt and pepper:

Kale, ground turkey (or any protein/tofu grounds) and onion

Spinach, ahi tuna (or chicken) and balsamic vinaigrette

Cauliflower rice, curry sauce and shrimp

If you don't eat seafood / meat you can sub all of these out for delicious tofu grounds. I call these LAZY (but still GAF) BOWLS, ya welcome.

Setting plans like a menu and opening up your creativity can tap into your confidence and discipline to stay consistent. It starts off with something as small as planning and making a dish to establish that feeling of accomplishment. Ultimately it becomes a contribution to your higher self.

YASSSSSSSSSS!

But really, this is what it's about, rebuilding or continuing to build to that higher self. Everything you do starts with the time and effort you take for you and your mental health, which brings me to the next chapter...

BUT FIRST, an exercise: Write out a menu for the week. You can use the next few pages to put down your grocery lists, track your calories for the week or write down reminders of new dishes to try. DO YOU, here's some space to do it.

_____

_____

_____

_____

_____

_____

_____

_____

_____

_____

_____

_____

_____

_____

_____

_____

_____

_____

_____

_____

_____

_____

_____

_____

_____

"During your life never stop dreaming, No one can take away your dreams." – Tupac

---

GAF = GET AFTER FITNESS

I can't stress enough how exercising and conscious breathing benefit your body and mind for the better. Exercising is essential to balancing a healthy life style and brain stimulation. Endorphins released during a workout also relieve stress and for every hour you do work out, your adding about a day to your life span. **HELLO INCENTIVE.**

So let's get into WTF works for you

For me, just walking into a gym is a hell no. I need more incentive; a community of people struggling with me, an allotted time period AND someone telling me what to do. High maintenance? Maybe, but I also know what will motivate me to stay consistent.

I found a program that works exactly for me and gets me excited about working out. It's a high interval training setting, with a group of people and it lasts an hour.

Let's be realistic, when I first got back into the groove of incorporating exercise into my life, while balancing a career, it was a slow start. I worked out maybe two times a week and slowly worked my way up to four or five. SO let's remove the pressure that you have to go from zero to Teyana Taylor in like a week, because that's not happening and with anything great (LIKE YA BODY) it's going to take time.

Start off exploring

Are you curious about trying any new classes? Usually the first class or gym session is free or at a very low cost. Don't give me that BS you don't have an hour to go this week. Pick a day, write it down and stick to it. There are so many options out there; Kickboxing, yoga, high interval workouts, cross-fit, taking a walk. **DO SOMETHING** for thirty minutes or more at least twice this week.

If you have any type of tracker

An Apple watch, Fitbit, a piece of paper, hello, these very pages, please use it. Writing down a class time or day will re-enforce the promise to yourself; but tracking it is the treat when you're done or even write down what you did in class, like this...

"Tried a 45 minute Zumba class today, high energy loved the play list and felt great after"

You're now associating an accomplishment with positivity and igniting the incentive to do it again and again.
On the flip side seeing the "calories burned" number light across the screen on your device

is something to be proud of and post to your social media story AMIRIGHT?

Exercise: Use the next few pages to hold yourself accountable for the classes you plan to take and how you feel about each one after. Track your exercise. We're building up that accountability, self-love and ... muscles.

_____
_____
_____
_____
_____
_____
_____
_____
_____
_____
_____
_____
_____
_____
_____
_____
_____
_____
_____
_____
_____
_____
_____
_____

_____
_____
_____
_____
_____
_____
_____
_____
_____
_____
_____

*"I'ma keep running
'cause a winner don't
quit on themselves." –
Beyonce*

_____
_____
_____
_____
_____
_____
_____
_____
_____
_____
_____
_____
_____
_____
_____

_____
_____
_____
_____
_____
_____
_____
_____
_____
_____

"If at first you don't succeed, dust yourself off and try again." - Aaliyah

_____
_____
_____
_____
_____
_____
_____
_____
_____
_____
_____
_____
_____
_____
_____
_____
_____

GAF = GET ALL FRIENDS/FAMILY

Get your friends (and/or family) together and let them know how much you appreciate them. Having a support system is so important and having real friends who are invested in your ideas and who are about you can be so inspiring and make all the difference. Take the time to express gratitude. Reflect on a few aspects of your life where your friends/family have been there for you.

Now, while trying to express gratitude if you come across a moment where it's a little harder to pinpoint what your friend has done for you, or you for them, then maybe its time to move that energy to a more positive entity. Feel me?

Whether your support group is big or small, let them know you're working on becoming a better person. Communicating this can influence them to do the same. This communication can add another layer to your accountability. At the very least it communicates why you might be skipping out on a weekend of drinks, why you're saving a little extra money or meditating a little more. We want to attract as much positivity and light to ourselves as possible.

While maintaining positive relationships the real key here, is time management. Let's write a list of what we need to pull back on and push for. Here are a few examples...

I need to pull back on:
Screen time
Weekend drinks
Eating take out

How do I do that?

Screen time - Set a timer on your phone that alarms you after 20 minutes of screen time. Have a replacement; write in your *Self Help Guide to GAF* when you want to go on social media. Write out the time.

Weekend drinks – Again, time yourself; give yourself a curfew that will naturally give your self a drink limit. Viola! One aspect of your life where you have saved time and money

Eating take out - We already talked about spending more at the grocery store than eating take out. If it's a treat yourself day, then by all means TREAT YOSELF. If it isn't, have a bite at home before you go out. Order an appetizer or split with a friend if you feel a strong desire to order something.

How much time do you spend texting or on the phone when you could be doing something else?

The rule I use is; if a text is getting too heated or you find yourself sending over **five lines** of text to someone; end the text or just CALL. Yes I said it. Call someone. Text was not built for in depth conceptual conversations. You can't hear the influx of someone's voice or how they're responding to you. Emojis just don't do it sometimes. We're trying to keep the positivity flowing. CALL - explain yourself or find out what the person really means. Diffuse the situation and keep it pushing. It's healthier to do that rather than sitting there wondering, assuming, blocking your creativity and taking the **TIME** and mental capacity it takes to conjure up an unnecessarily long message and then waiting for the reply, nah sis (bruh). We don't need negative spaces, especially from a text. Ew.

Exercises: Write out what you appreciate about your friends/family. Figure out areas in your life where you can take more time for you to get to your higher self.

_____

_____

_____

_____

_____

_____

_____

_____

_____

_____

_____

_____

_____

_____

_____

_____

_____

_____

_____

_____

_____

_____

_____

_____

_____

_____

_____

"Don't text me, tell it straight to my face."-Lizzo

_____

_____

_____

_____

_____

_____

_____

_____

_____

_____

_____

_____

_____

*"Looking in the mirror I
thank God for what I'm
bout to be."- Saweetie*

_____

_____

_____

_____

_____

_____

_____

_____

_____

_____

_____

_____

_____

_____

_____

GAF = **G**RATITUDE **A**LWAYS **F**ULFILLS

This is pretty self explanatory and so true. Appreciating what is going well in your life will only prompt you to gravitate toward more positivity and abundance.

It's important to appreciate where you are at this very moment, mentally and physically. Look over yourself, what do you love about YOU, right now?

Think about that for a second. Really feel that love and appreciation, for yourself, and you'll want to continue to nurture it and bring that feeling to a new level. Do you love your; hair, lips, nails? Are you funny? Do you have a great smile? Are you vivacious or a thoughtful person?

Appreciating the external and internal components that make you, you, can boost your confidence. It can also make you realize how you can incorporate these attributes into your daily life, career and purpose with others.

Next, turn your complaints into gratitude. For example, if you've been complaining about not making enough money. Instead, shift that focus to the money you do have and what it has allowed you to do. Pay bills? Buy Clothes? Food?

Yes! Thank you Money!

Exercise: Write out what you love about yourself and where you can incorporate your attributes daily! Find at least five complaints you can turn into gratitude!

_____
_____
_____
_____
_____
_____
_____
_____
_____
_____
_____
_____
_____
_____
_____
_____
_____
_____
_____
_____
_____
_____
_____
_____
_____
_____

_____
_____
_____
_____
_____
_____
_____
_____
_____
_____
_____

"None of my fears can go where I'm headed." – Beyonce

_____
_____
_____
_____
_____
_____
_____
_____
_____
_____
_____
_____
_____
_____
_____
_____

GAF = GET A FUTURE

Everything takes consistency including working toward your vision. So let's start there, do you have one?

Where do you see yourself in a year from now or five? Take a moment and reflect on that, truly, and I promise you'll start moving differently and with intention when you see the light at the end of the tunnel.

Write it down in the next few pages and be extremely specific. Whether you go back to revisit these goals daily, weekly or monthly subconsciously your mind starts to work toward these goals.

A painter can't start their work without inspiration. Without a thought or emotion they're trying to evoke or a scene they can envision - the canvas stays blank. It's the same for life. What's in your heart? Is there a passion, something more you would like to learn or explore? How far will you take your career and how do you plan to inspire someone else?

This thought process is exactly how I came to my career, my purpose, to this workbook, and everything I plan to do. My plan is always a pull toward a vision and my purpose is always a hopeful impact on others. Every single step is an expression of gratitude and then I move forward to the next one. GAF, it's the best you can do for yourself.

_____
_____
_____
_____
_____
_____
_____
_____
_____
_____
_____
_____
_____
_____
_____
_____
_____
_____
_____
_____
_____
_____
_____
_____
_____
_____

_____

_____

_____

_____

_____

_____

_____

_____

_____

"The best thing you can do for a person is inspire them." – Nipsey Hussle

_____

_____

_____

_____

_____

_____

_____

_____

_____

_____